TABLE OF CONTENTS

Page

ACRONYMS

ADP	Army Doctrinal Publication
ADRP	Army Doctrinal Reference Publication
AQ	Al Qaeda
AQAP	Al Qaeda Arabian Peninsula
AQI	Al Qaeda in Iraq
BVSR	Blind Variation Selective Retention
CRS	Congressional Research Service
JP	Joint Publication
OODA	Observe, Orient, Decide, and Act
SAMS	School of Advanced Military Studies
USACGSC	United States Army Command and General Staff College

ILLUSTRATIONS

INTRODUCTION

> Although our intellect always longs for clarity and certainty, our nature often finds uncertainty fascinating.[1]
>
> —Clausewitz, *On War*, Book One, Chapter 1

The operational and strategic environment that the United States Armed Forces will operate in has grown increasingly interconnected and complex characterized by novelty, uncertainty, and ambiguity. Joint Publication (JP) 3-0, *Joint Operations,* describes the strategic environment as uncertain, complex, rapidly changing and requiring persistent engagement. It characterizes the environment as "fluid" with conditions that continually change, such as changing alliances, partnerships, and the emergence of novel national and transnational threats. JP 3-0, concludes that uncertainty, ambiguity, and surprise will dominate regional and global events and severely limit our ability to predict with reliable accuracy what security challenges will emerge in the future.[2] Despite some of the new emerging circumstances and conditions of the environment, the characteristics of uncertainty, unpredictability, novelty and perpetual change in the environment are not new features to military endeavors and war.

Carl von Clausewitz in his famous book *On War* characterizes war as "more than a true chameleon" due to its unpredictability.[3] Throughout Chapter One, Clausewitz emphasizes the imperfection of knowledge, the assessing of probabilities, and the role of chance in the conduct of

---

[1] Carl von Clausewitz, *On War,* trans. Michael Howard and Peter Paret (Princeton, NJ: Princeton University Press, 1976), 86.

[2] Chairman, Joint Chiefs of Staff, Joint Publication (JP) 3-0, *Joint Operations* (Washington, DC: Government Printing Office, 2011), I-2.

[3] Clausewitz, *On War*, 89.

war.[4] Clausewitz uses the term chance to refer to the unpredictability inherent to war and this element forms one part of his famous "trinity" of war. Former Air Force Colonel John Boyd in his essay, *Destruction and Creation,* describes uncertainty as a fundamental and irresolvable characteristic of our lives.[5] Boyd goes on to suggest that adaptability counters uncertainty because it allows systems to adjust to it.[6]

William Ross Ashby, in *Design for a Brain,* used the physical process of equilibrium as an analogy for adaptive behavior.[7] By establishing this analogy, Ashby describes adaptive behavior with the language and mathematical rigor used to describe physical systems in states of equilibrium.[8] While using a mechanistic process as an analogy, Ashby acknowledges that learning and being able to change a system's organization and structure distinguishes the adaptive processes of living systems from purely mechanistic ones.[9] In Ashby's model, systems regulate variety of a few certain *essential variables* to maintain equilibrium.[10] Cybernetics models the interactions of these systems with each other as control loops interacting with one another. In this control relation, regulation requires that the system have more of an effect on the environment than the environment has on the system, to include the other systems in the environment, referred

---

[4]Ibid., 85.

[5]Frans P. B. Osinga, *Science, Strategy and War the Strategic Theory of John Boyd* (New York: Routledge, 2007), 1.

[6]Ibid., 172.

[7]W. Ross Ashby, *Design for a Brain; the Origin of Adaptive Behavior* (New York: Wiley, 1960), 1.

[8]Ibid.

[9]Ibid., 1-2.

[10]Ibid., 2-10.

to hereafter as the object.[11] Cybernetics systems achieve these asymmetries in the control loop to attain relative advantageous states at equilibrium by strengthening the system and by weakening the influence of the environment through effective regulation.[12]

This study proposes first that adaptive processes are Markov processes and follows the Markov convergence theorem. A Markov process is a stochastic process that has a finite number of states, fixed transition probabilities, the possibility of getting from any state to another through a series of transitions, and does not produce a simple cycle.[13] The Markov Convergence theorem states a system following a Markov Process will eventually reach a *statistical* equilibrium.[14] This study proposes what distinguishes the adaptive processes of living, goal seeking systems is they can change the fixed transition probabilities through learning to produce asymmetry in a control relation at equilibrium. The study concluded that learning in living, goal seeking systems creates the asymmetry in the control loop versus direct regulation which may produce an interim state change, but not produce changes in the relative state at eventual equilibrium. Second, the study found that the step of representation of the external situation and environment drives and guides what the system learns and adapts to and that uncertainty guides and provides the drive for learning, variety, change, and adaptability. As the system gains more knowledge, uncertainty increases because the possibilities increase in the mind of the observer. Finally, the study found that goal seeking systems do not have just a single goal, but a range of goals and they possess the

---

[11]Francis Heylighen and Cliff Joslyn, "Cybernetics and Second Order Cybernetics," *Encyclopedia of Physical Science & Technology*, ed. R.A. Myers, 3rd ed., vol. 4 (New York: Academic Press, 2001), 17.

[12]Ibid.

[13]Scott E. Page, "Markov Processes," n.d., 70-74, http://vserver1.cscs.lsa.umich.edu/~spage/ONLINECOURSE/R10Markov.pdf (accessed 4 April 2014).

[14]Ibid., 70–75.

capacity of adjusting these goals or determining new goals.[15] Which means, a system can achieve regulation when disturbances threaten a system's essential variables by *adapting* its goals, so that the threatened variables are no longer threatened or essential.[16] Therefore as systems adapt to disturbances in this manner, they adapt and change their essential variables and achieve asymmetry by assuming a state that potentially resets the selection criteria for fitness.

Cybernetics defines variety as the measure of the number of distinct states a system can be in.[17] Cybernetics defines regulation, referred also as control or selection, as the reduction of variety.[18] The set of all possible states that a system can be in defines its state space[19] or, as Ashby would refer to it, product space.[20] So variety serves as a quantitative measure for this state space. Variety also generates uncertainty about the state of the system at a particular point in time and when variety occurs in a process, it creates uncertainty in the outcomes of that process.[21] Which means that variety also serves as a measure for uncertainty.[22] Therefore, organization and constraints to variety reduces uncertainty. Ashby sought these constraints or interaction rules, in the form of laws and principles, which reduced the potentially unlimited possible variety that

---

[15]Heylighen and Joslyn, "Cybernetics and Second Order Cybernetics," 13.

[16]W. Ross Ashby, *An Introduction to Cybernetics* (New York: J. Wiley, 1956), 247.

[17]Cliff Joslyn and Francis Heylighen, "Variety," Principia Cybernetica Web, 2001, http://pespmc1.vub.ac.be/ VARIETY.html (accessed 13 April 2014).

[18]Heylighen and Joslyn, "Cybernetics and Second Order Cybernetics," 15.

[19]Joslyn and Heylighen, "Variety."

[20]R. Ashby and J. Goldstein, "Principles of Self-Organizing Systems (Originally Published in 1962)," *Emergence : Complexity and Organization* 6, no. 1/2 (2004): 105.

[21]Joslyn and Heylighen, "Variety."

[22]Heylighen and Joslyn, "Cybernetics and Second Order Cybernetics," 6.

could be imagined to the variety that could be observed.[23] Ashby states the product space, which encompasses all of the possibilities in the mind of the observer, not the environment, produces uncertainty.[24] This description leads to a counterintuitive conclusion that more knowledge or information available to a system increases the uncertainty of a system because it increases the possibilities that exist. Therefore, the appropriate selection or constraint of information reduces uncertainty. Another counterintuitive conclusion is that adaptability necessarily requires uncertainty. Uncertainty creates the need for systems to learn and produce the requisite variety to maintain equilibrium with a changing environment. Karl Wieck notes that certainty can constrain and even inhibit action, to include the ability to adapt.[25] Wieck states that plausibility, not certainty and accuracy, drives and guides learning.[26] Goal-seeking, adaptive systems achieve a favorable equilibrium with their environment through learning.

The Merriam Webster dictionary defines equilibrium as a condition when all competing or opposing force or influences are balanced.[27] Describing the competing influences in the terms of variety, the system could be described as being in equilibrium when the variety of the system is balanced with the variety in the environment. Cybernetics defines a disturbance, also referred to as a perturbation, as any effect that moves the system away from equilibrium and can originate

---

[23]S. A. Umpleby, "Ross Ashby's General Theory of Adaptive Systems," *International Journal of General Systems* 38, no. 2 (2009): 233.

[24]Ashby and Goldstein, "Principles of Self-Organizing Systems," 105.

[25]Karl E. Weick, *Sensemaking in Organizations* (Thousand Oaks: Sage Publications, 1995), 59–61.

[26]Karl E. Weick, "Organizing and Sensemaking," *Organizational Behavior* 2 (2006): 419.

[27]Free Merriam-Webster Dictionary, s.v. "Equilibrium," http://www.merriam-webster.com/dictionary/equilibrium (accessed 7 April 2014).

internally or externally from the system.[28] The strength of the disturbance is measured by the

transient, the effects in terms of state change on a system, the duration of the transient, and

whether the transient produces a permanent change.[29] Goal-seeking implies the ability of a

system to regulate these disturbances to achieve preferred state or favorable equilibrium.[30] Ashby

describes here the dynamic nature of equilibrium.

> Firstly, we notice that ''stable equilibrium'' does not mean immobility. A body,
> e.g. a pendulum swinging, may vary considerably and yet be in stable equilibrium the
> whole time. Secondly, we note that the concept of ''equilibrium'' is essentially a
> dynamic one. If we just look at the three bodies [cube, cone, and sphere] on our table and
> do nothing with them the concept of equilibrium can hardly be said to have any particular
> meaning. It is only when we disturb the bodies and observes their subsequent reactions
> that the concept develops its full meaning.[31]

Ashby further refines the definition of a stable equilibrium as one in which a system will return to

the equilibrium state even when some of its variables are disturbed slightly. To illustrate the

variance between stable and unstable equilibrium in systems, Ashby used the example of the

three bodies of a cube, cone, and sphere. A cube resting on a table will return to the same state

even if disturbed and tilted. Conversely, while possible to balance a cone on its point, the slightest

disturbance will cause it to fall into a remote state and will not return to the balanced state without

external intervention. The sphere represents an equilibrium capable of being stable at many

adjacent states and can be moved freely between those states.[32] Taken from another perspective,

these particular states of equilibrium also illustrates what author, Nassim Taleb, has described as

[28]Chris Lucas, "Perturbation and Transients—The Edge of Chaos," 2005,
http://www.calresco.org/perturb.htm. (accessed 7 April 2014).

[29]Joslyn and Heylighen, "Variety."

[30]Heylighen and Joslyn, "Cybernetics and Second Order Cybernetics," 12.

[31]Peter M Asaro, "From Mechanisms of Adaptation to Intelligence Amplifiers: The
Philosophy of W. Ross Ashby," *Mechanical Mind in History* (2008): 156.

[32]Ibid.

robust, fragile, and anti-fragile systems.[33] The "cube" equilibrium represents the robust system where disturbances do not improve or degrade the system, it returns to the same relative equilibrium point. The "cone" equilibrium represents the fragile system where the slightest disturbance will push it out of equilibrium and cannot return without external intervention. The "sphere" equilibrium represents antifragile systems, since it can move freely between many adjacent states in response to disturbances and therefore have the ability to find better, more optimal states. Meaning a system with a "sphere" equilibrium is better suited for adaptation in a complex and ever changing environment as it can freely assume the necessary states until it achieves regulation. Effective regulation and learning enables systems to establish a state with a favorable equilibrium.

Regulation reduces the variety to maintain a desired goal or equilibrium and an autonomous system's most fundamental goal is survival and the maintenance of its essential organization.[34] However, as mentioned previously, a system can also have a range of acceptable states as its goal, each with its own associated *essential variables*, the variables and dimensions defining these relative preferred states. Therefore, a system must keep these variable within an acceptable range in order to achieve one of their preferred states.[35] Which means that the essential variables may differ depending on the preferred state or goal selected by the system. This goal can be defined as a gradient, or fitness function, which defines the degree of value or preference of one state relative to another.[36] Therefore, autonomous, goal-seeking, equifinal systems requires

---

[33]Nassim Nicholas Taleb, *Antifragile: Things That Gain from Disorder* (New York: Random House, 2012), 1–10.

[34]Heylighen and Joslyn, "Cybernetics and Second Order Cybernetics," 12.

[35]Ibid., 13.

[36]Ibid.

regulation and therefore regulation becomes one of ongoing adaptation to optimize or maximize fitness.[37]

According to cybernetics, the system can regulate the variety in the environment in several ways. First the system can directly regulate the variety in the environment or the disturbance.[38] Second, the system can learn and adapt to increase the capacity of the regulator or control system to better regulate their environment.[39] Third, the system can change or shape their environment so that new interaction rules emerge and lead to the desired state for both the system.[40] Finally, Ashby offers a fourth alternative where systems can achieve regulations by changing its goals or preferred state so that its essential variables are no longer threatened or the threatened variables are no longer essential, usually through the lowering of aspiration.[41] While Ashby expressed this change to achieve regulation as a lowering of standards and expectations of a system's goals, this method of regulation potentially represents another means of gaining asymmetry, as adaptive systems may adapt to a novel form that resets the selection criteria for fitness determination.

The study will begin with the summary of relevant concepts drawn from Ashby's major bodies of work and current cybernetic thought regarding adaptation, learning, and regulation. Utilizing these basic concepts, the study will model and analyze the interaction between the control loops of adaptive systems as a Markov process which results in an equilibrium of requisite variety. The study will then examine the case studies of Napoleon's *Grand Armee* in the

---

[37]Ibid.

[38]Umpleby, "Ross Ashby's General Theory of Adaptive Systems," 236–238.

[39]Ashby, *An Introduction to Cybernetics*, 246–247.

[40]Umpleby, "Ross Ashby's General Theory of Adaptive Systems," 236–238.

[41]Ashby, *An Introduction to Cybernetics*, 246–247.

Jena-Auerstadt campaign of 1806 and present day Al Qaeda to analyze how these systems learned and adjusted their organization and structure to achieve regulation.

LITERATURE REVIEW

William Ross Ashby

Antoine Bousquet proposes the theories of complexity and chaos, referred to collectively as "chaoplexity," serves as that corpus of current scientific thought.[42] However, cybernetics contributed significantly to the conceptual and theoretical foundation of both Chaos and Complexity theory in 1970s and 1980s.[43] Cybernetics, as a science, studies the abstract principles of organization in complex systems and focuses on how systems function with the properties of other systems independent of their material or constituents components. Derived from the Greek word *kybernetes,* or "steersman," cybernetics describes goal directedness or how systems move towards and maintain their goals, while countering disturbances from their environment, which also include internally generated disturbances.[44] Ashby, considered one of the founders of cybernetic thought, contributed much to the development of the foundational concepts of cybernetics and complexity theory.[45] The use of concepts that Ashby conceived in the 1950s, such as the equilibrium model for adaptation, complex systems, artificial intelligence, and the Law of Requisite Variety, still remain very relevant today and clearly shows the robustness of his thought and applicability even in the modern context.

---

[42]Antoine J Bousquet, *The Scientific Way of Warfare: Order and Chaos on the Battlefields of Modernity* (New York: Columbia University Press, 2009), 67.

[43]Ibid., 118–119.

[44]Heylighen and Joslyn, "Cybernetics and Second Order Cybernetics," 2–3.

[45]Ibid.

Organized complexity, such as brains, organisms, societies, and the dynamics of behavior interested Ashby and focused on the functional aspects of and the adaptive behavior in living, dynamic systems.[46] In *Design for a Brain: The Origin of Adaptive Behavior,* Ashby explained and described the adaptive processes of living, goal seeking systems and set out much of his core concepts that he would develop throughout the remainder of his study. In *Design for a Brain,* Ashby equates adaptation to the physical process of equilibrium and he sought to show a system can be both mechanistic in nature and produce adaptive behavior.[47] Ashby would describe that the difference between living and machines that are purely mechanistic is the ability to learn behaviors from interacting with their environment and then adjust their structure or behavior to achieve equilibrium.[48] Through this analogy, Ashby explains that the adaptive behaviors could be analyzed and studied in the same manner as mechanical processes, independent of its specific material composition.[49] Ashby reasoned this meant that adaptive behaviors could now be described with the language and mathematical rigor of physical systems.[50] Despite the analogy to a mechanistic process, Ashby highlights a living adaptive system's ability to learn from its environment and adjust their structure and organization distinguishes it from purely mechanistic adaptive processes.[51] Later in the book, Ashby would describe two feedback loops for adaptive behavior. The first feedback loop operates frequently and makes small corrections to enable a

---

[46]Umpleby, "Ross Ashby's General Theory of Adaptive Systems," 283.

[47]Ashby, *Design for a Brain; the Origin of Adaptive Behavior*, 1.

[48]Asaro, "From Mechanisms of Adaptation to Intelligence Amplifiers," 154–156.

[49]Ibid., 154–155.

[50]Ibid., 155–156.

[51]Ibid., 156–158.

system to learn a pattern of appropriate behavior for a particular context or environment.[52] The second feedback loop operates less frequently and changes the structure of the system when the *essential variables* get pushed outside of limits and prevents the system from achieving its goal.[53] This second loop allows the system to learn that the change in the environment requires a new pattern of behavior to achieve the system's desired goal in order to survive.[54] The most fundamental goal of a system is survival and the preservation of its essential organization.[55] Ashby states as systems became more complex, their ability to learn and adjust to their environment would lessen the control that genetics have on their behavior.[56]

The next fundamental principle from Ashby articulated in this passage from Ashby's *Principles of the Self-Organizing System* describes self-organization at the most basic level:

> We start with the fact that systems in general go to equilibrium. Now most of a system's states are non-equilibrial [...] So in going from any state to one of the equilibria, the system is going from a larger number of states to a smaller one. In this way, it is performing a selection, in the purely objective sense that it rejects some states, by leaving them, and retains some other state, by sticking to it.[57]

While seemingly simple, this foundational principle contains many implications. It essentially states all stable systems go to equilibrium and as it does the variety in those systems decreases as it performs self-organization in the most basic sense. Variety in the system decreases as the system retains certain states, usually their preferred states, in favor of other states. This creates natural tension observed in goal directed system between variety for adaptation and stability.

---

[52]Umpleby, "Ross Ashby's General Theory of Adaptive Systems," 255–256.

[53]Ibid.

[54]Ibid.

[55]Heylighen and Joslyn, "Cybernetics and Second Order Cybernetics," 12.

[56]Ashby, *An Introduction to Cybernetics*, 212.

[57]Ashby and Goldstein, "Principles of Self-Organizing Systems," 118.

Faced with unlimited potential variations from the environment, systems would seek to maximize internal variety to be prepared for expected and unexpected contingencies, yet they constantly reduce variety in order to achieve stability and equilibrium. This would mean that the system would select and retain the requisite variety to maintain equilibrium. Related to this, Heylighen defined a *principle of asymmetric transitions*, which states that stable states have lower energy level, so minimal energy level in the system equates to stability.[58] This implies that the decrease in variety through organization equates to a lower state of energy. Drawing from this, Heylighen conceptualized energy as the capacity to do work or exert variety, making energy equivalent to potential variation or variety.[59] Which means, systems require energy to create variety, as either disturbance or internal variety. The more stable a system is the more energy will be required to move it from equilibrium. Additionally, regulation requires energy as the system reduces variety in the object or their own sub-systems by countering and destroying variety with variety.[60] So goal-seeking, open systems will maximally dissipate energy or variation in order to move to a more stable state by countering and destroying the variety from the environment that continually enters it to maintain stability.[61]

Ashby would express the equilibrium and the interaction between the system and the environment in terms of variety. Ashby describes variety as the means that systems communicated with one another.[62] Linking this with Heylighen's formulation of energy as

[58]Francis Heylighen, "Principles of Systems and Cybernetics: An Evolutionary Perspective," *Cybernetics and Systems* 92 (1992): 4–5.

[59]Ibid.

[60]Ashby, *An Introduction to Cybernetics*, 207.

[61]Francis Heylighen, "Principles of Systems and Cybernetics: An Evolutionary Perspective," 4–5.

[62]Ashby, *An Introduction to Cybernetics*, 210–211.

potential variation, systems interact with each other through the exchange of variety as work or energy and organization occurs when this communication occurs between elements.[63] Taken in whole, this means that the interaction between systems occurs through the exchange of variety, which in turn, implies that equilibrium between systems can be measured in terms of variety. Ashby would identify this interaction and communication between systems as a key factor in the formation of structure and organization of systems.[64]

In *Principles of the Self-Organizing System,* Ashby clarifies self-organization, a term which Ashby claims can lead to misunderstanding.[65] As defined by Ashby, self-organization is not about a system's propensity or ability for autonomous change, but refers to the system's ability to conduct selection to achieve a "good" organization relative to its environment.[66] The "self" in self-organization refers to the system and its environment as an inseparable whole.[67] Ashby states that organization by itself only requires conditionality between the parts and regularity in their behavior.[68] So without the context of its environment, a system's organization has no value in an absolute sense. Ashby describes self-organization as not as much going from unorganized to organized, but transforming from a "bad" organization to a "good" one. An organization's "goodness" is specific to the context of a given environment or circumstances.[69]

---

[63] Ashby and Goldstein, "Principles of Self-Organizing Systems," 104–106.

[64] Ibid., 105.

[65] Ibid., 113–115.

[66] Ibid., 114–117.

[67] Ibid., 117.

[68] Ibid., 110.

[69] Ibid., 114.

Which means, the relevance of the organization and its utility must be reestablished in every subsequent context.[70]

Ashby also introduced the concept of systems "breaking" using the analogy of a machine. Like a machine pushed beyond the limits of its design, Ashby describes a system breaking when it reaches a critical state after a disturbance drives its essential variables outside of acceptable ranges.[71] Ashby's asserts that while breaks in systems can be considered undesirable and a condition to be avoided, they provide a necessary mechanism for learning and fitness.[72] In self-organizing systems, the process of breaking and reorganization continues indefinitely until the essential variables are brought back within acceptable limits and equilibrium reestablished.[73] Since breaks represent a change of organization, all dynamic systems will change their internal organizations spontaneously until they reach some form of equilibrium.[74] The system becomes increasingly fit and stable once it adapts to the disturbance that "broke" it, since the system can maintain equilibrium in spite of the disturbance. Therefore, self-organization becomes learning and adaptation at the system's level. Heinz Von Foerster expanded on this notion introducing the *order from noise* principle which states that random low level disturbances or "noise" enhances system's self-organization.[75] In this manner, systems reach increasingly fit states by learning through smaller, manageable breaks that do not significantly disrupt the system's equilibrium.

---

[70]Ibid., 110.

[71]Ashby, *Design for a Brain; the Origin of Adaptive Behavior*, 85.

[72]Ibid.

[73]Asaro, "From Mechanisms of Adaptation to Intelligence Amplifiers," 159.

[74]Ibid.

[75]Heylighen and Joslyn, "Cybernetics and Second Order Cybernetics," 10.

Therefore, if we view self-organization as learning at the system's level, then Von Foerster's principle describes continual learning versus episodic learning.

An analogy with an ecological niche best illustrates Ashby's concept of self- organizing systems in equilibrium with each other as a bounded whole.[76] In ecology, a niche describes how an organism or population responds to the distribution of resources and competitors and how it in turn alters those same factors in an ecological system.[77] The fundamental niche defines the ideal conditions and the full spectrum of environmental factors that can be potentially utilized by a system that exists in the absence of interactions with other systems or the environment. The realized niche is the constrained subset of the fundamental niche resulting from interaction with the environment and other systems and includes constraints coming from historical factors, dispersion, competitors, and the realized environment.[78] The optimal goal of those within the niche would be to maximize their realized niche in relation to their competitors through the pursuit of higher fitness.[79] This analogy illustrates why Ashby felt the term "self" organization could be misleading as the system does not itself determine its realized niche, but requires the interaction with the environment and the other systems in the niche to determine requisite variety. The system thus self-organizes to their environment and pursues higher fitness through regulation, by selecting the requisite variety that provides the most favorable state at equilibrium relative to its environment, while denying the same to their competitors.

---

[76]Ashby and Goldstein, "Principles of Self-Organizing Systems," 117.

[77]University of Colorado at Boulder, "Understanding Our Environment - Niche_Modelling.pdf," n.d., http://culter.colorado.edu/~kittel/Biogeog_lectures/L4b_niche/ Niche_Modelling.pdf (accessed 4 April 2014).

[78]Ibid.

[79]Ibid.

Ashby states that the Law of Requisite Variety is a measure for regulation.[80] The most common formulation of this law, states the variety available to a regulator must be equal to or larger than the variety of the disturbances in order to maintain stability or equilibrium.[81] Still, Ashby acknowledges that the regulator necessarily has less variety than the potentially limitless possibilities of variety in the environment.[82] A later more specific cybernetic formulation of the Law of Requisite Variety states the larger the variety in the regulator, then the higher the probability that one of those states can counter the disturbance before it affects the system.[83]

Ashby explains that self-organized systems can maintain equilibrium in spite of the potentially unlimited variety in the environment because the system only compensates for the disturbances that affect a relatively small number of the system's variables.[84] Which means that the equilibrium of autonomous, living system can be dynamic and not uniform over the overall system.[85] The living system can maintain the essential variables of its organization in equilibrium even as the rest of the system "breaks" and dynamically adapts to the disturbances to achieve the desired equilibrium.[86] From this, Ashby would develop his conceptualization of ultra stability, the ability of systems to find a suitable equilibrium regardless of the changes in its environment,[87] and of multi-stability, which is an ultrastable system composed of multiple and dispersed

---

[80]Ashby, *An Introduction to Cybernetics*, 207.

[81]Ibid.

[82]Ibid.

[83]Heylighen, "Principles of Systems and Cybernetics: An Evolutionary Perspective," 7.

[84]Ashby, *Design for a Brain; the Origin of Adaptive Behavior*, 62–65.

[85]Asaro, "From Mechanisms of Adaptation to Intelligence Amplifiers," 160.

[86]Ibid.

[87]Ibid.

ultrastable subsystems, each of which can maintain the essential variable even as other points become unstable and change.[88] This allows the system to adapt more rapidly as more of the system can change without the loss of equilibrium or more robust and maintain stability when confronted with disturbances. Similarly, the more variety a system possesses the higher the probability it will have the requisite variety or take less time and energy to transition to a desired state or organization.[89] With inappropriate variety then the system may take too much time to go through the transitions to assume a state capable of dealing with the situation or disturbance.[90] Therefore, requisite variety implies a system must not just have variety, it must have the right kind of variety, to cope with its environment. With an environment that increases in complexity and the regulator constrained by a finite capacity of variety, the selection of the requisite variety becomes even more important.[91]

Ashby states the regulator possesses a finite capacity for variety by drawing a parallel to Shannon's 10th theorem, which states the finite capacity of the channel constrains the amount of noise it can remove from a signal.[92] Therefore, a system's finite capacity for variety constrains the amount of variety it can regulate.[93] Unlike Information Theory which deals with contexts rich in signal with relative small fraction of noise, Ashby observes that goal-seeking adaptive systems face the opposite situation with the context rich with disturbing errors and noise and sparse in

---

[88] Ashby, *Design for a Brain; the Origin of Adaptive Behavior*, 170–173.

[89] Heylighen, "Principles of Systems and Cybernetics: An Evolutionary Perspective," 4–5.

[90] Ashby and Goldstein, "Principles of Self-Organizing Systems," 113.

[91] Ashby, *An Introduction to Cybernetics*, 245.

[92] Ibid.

[93] Ibid.

signal.[94] Which means, selecting and retaining the variety that best achieves its goal and preferred states for a system becomes even more important when dealing with complex systems. Thus, possessing the requisite variety of actions or states alone cannot achieve effective regulation. The system must also have the requisite knowledge to select the correct variety in a situation.[95]

The *principle of requisite knowledge* states the system must have the knowledge to select the appropriate variety to achieve effective regulation.[96] Without knowledge, the system would have to resort to blind variation and the larger the variety of possible disturbances, the smaller the probability that blind variation will produce the requisite variety.[97] When a system produces variety through *blind variation*, systems do so without the foreknowledge of which variations or organizations produced will be successful or selected.[98] Essentially, blind variation is the system's equivalent of trial and error and the source for novelty. The basic blind variation and selective retention (BVSR) mechanism begins with blind variation producing a variety of states and as they produce a stable behavior or state, the system selects and retains them.[99] Heylighen did note that some systems do not attempt things blindly, but have some expectations of what will work and vicariously selects those states or actions. Heylighen concludes that previous blind variations selected and retained by the system produces this "knowledge" to conduct vicarious selection.[100] Therefore, learning reduces uncertainty through previous knowledge or retention in

---

[94] Ashby, *An Introduction to Cybernetics*, 273–274.

[95] Heylighen, "Principles of Systems and Cybernetics: An Evolutionary Perspective," 9.

[96] Ibid.

[97] Ibid., 6.

[98] Ibid.

[99] Ibid.

[100] Ibid.

memory of successful blind variations and allows the system to anticipate and perform more effective selection of requisite variety.[101]

The *principle of incomplete knowledge* simply states that the system can never have complete knowledge or representation of an infinitely more complex environment. Which means that the representations must necessarily be incomplete and simpler that the reality that they represent.[102] Otherwise the variation and selection processes would take as much time as the real world, precluding any anticipation and regulation.[103] Additionally, the more variety a system has to select from, the more complex the requisite knowledge must be to select the requisite variety.[104] Having established that blind variation has an increasingly smaller probability of producing the requisite variety as the potential variation of disturbances increase and the finite capacity for variety of the regulator, the system must now develop the means to select the best representation, knowledge, and variety to achieve regulation and the system's goals.

In a complex environment, once the capacity of a regulator has been reached, another control loop will need to form over it to control the residual variety. The hierarchical levels will continue to form in this manner until it achieves regulation.[105] The formation of additional hierarchical levels can also hinder control as more levels the signals and actions passes through, the higher the probability they will suffer from noise, corruption, or delays.[106] *Aulin's law of requisite hierarchy* states the required number of levels depends on the regulatory ability of the

---

[101]Ibid., 6–7.

[102]Ibid., 9.

[103]Ibid.

[104]Ibid., 8–9.

[105]Heylighen and Joslyn, "Cybernetics and Second Order Cybernetics," 18.

[106]Ibid.

19

regulator at any given level. Meaning, the weaker the regulatory ability of a given level, the more hierarchy or levels will be required to achieve regulation.[107] Which means, systems should maximize the regulatory ability at each level to the extent allowable by the Law of Requisite Variety and minimize the requisite layers of hierarchy.[108] When variety eventually exceeds that capacity, the system must necessarily undergo a process called by cyberneticist Valentin Turchin as *metasystem transition* to produce a higher control level to allow the system to progress.[109]

In complex regulators as hierarchical levels form, goals are typically arranged in this hierarchy, where the higher level goals control the settings for the subsystem goals, by making them dependent on them.[110] This means, if the variety coming from the environment no longer requires the additional hierarchical levels, the potential and propensity increases for goals to become impeded or distorted.[111] Ashby stated that adaptation becomes impeded if the organization of the system is not aligned with the context of the environment.[112] If too little structure then the system may take too much time to go through the transitions to aggregate to the required level of complexity to deal with the situation or disturbance.[113] Too much structure, then the system may not adapt fast enough relative to the environment.[114] Boyd offers similar insights on effects and the different time horizons as each level of an organization has its own Observe,

---

[107]Ibid.

[108]Ashby, *An Introduction to Cybernetics.*, 245.

[109]Heylighen and Joslyn, "Cybernetics and Second Order Cybernetics," 18.

[110]Ibid., 17.

[111]Ibid., 17–18.

[112]Ashby and Goldstein, "Principles of Self-Organizing Systems," 113.

[113]Ibid.

[114]Ibid.

Orient, Decide, and Act (OODA) loop cycle time and which increases as the levels of organization and the number of events it has to deal with increases.[115]

Ashby equated intellectual power as being the equivalent of appropriate selection or regulation of variety. Therefore, problem solving and learning becomes a matter of appropriate selection and retention.[116] The identification of constraints, arrangement, organization, and hierarchy enhances the intelligence of the system.[117] This enhanced intelligence produces an improved representation of the external situation, which in turn allows the system to conduct better selection. Boyd also stated the importance of having a repertoire of orientation patterns and to select the correct one according to the situation at hand, while denying that ability to the enemy.[118]

---

[115]Osinga, *Science, Strategy and War the Strategic Theory of John Boyd*, 155.

[116]Ashby, *An Introduction to Cybernetics*, 272.

[117]Ibid., 272.

[118]Osinga, *Science, Strategy and War the Strategic Theory of John Boyd*, 236–237.

Cybernetic Models of Regulation

Figure 1: Basic Mechanisms of Regulation.

Source: Heylighen and Joslyn, "Cybernetics and Second Order Cybernetics," 14.

The basic mechanisms for regulation prevent the variety from disturbances from affecting the system's essential variables. The basic mechanisms are listed in Figure 1 from left to right: buffering, feedforward, and feedback. In each case, the effect of disturbances *D* on the essential variables *E* is reduced or blocked by a passive buffer *B*, or by an active Regulator *R*.[119] Viewed from another perspective, these basic mechanisms regulates learning at the system's level.

Buffering passively reduces or blocks the effects of a disturbance on a system without active intervention, but unlike feedback, it does not actively change or improve a system's state.[120] This means buffering mechanisms protect the equilibrium of the system, but it does not improve the system and it may impede learning by blocking the variety coming from the environment before the system can form an accurate representation of it. Therefore, too much buffering can impede a system's ability to adapt and leads to episodic learning and surprise.

---

[119]Heylighen and Joslyn, "Cybernetics and Second Order Cybernetics," 13-14.

[120]Ibid., 13.

Black swans, defined by author Nassim Taleb as a rare, improbable event that has extreme consequences or effects, are examples of the effects of too much buffering on a system.[121]

Cybernetics defines feedforward as cause regulating mechanisms which anticipates and tries to regulate disturbances before it has a chance to affect the system's essential variables.[122] The feedforward mechanism requires requisite knowledge to both anticipate the disturbance and the effect it will have on the system's variable.[123] Which means, this mechanism controls the variety in the environment in order to counter or shape select potential disturbances or the systems that produces them.[124] Therefore, a regulator would need to form an accurate representation of the current situation to vicariously carry out the requisite selection in anticipation of certain conditions. Anticipatory selection mitigates for inadequate internal variations or requisite variety, since the regulator will counter it prior to it affecting the system's essential variables.[125] However, no regulator will ever have complete information and anticipate all future possibilities, meaning that the regulator will necessarily make errors. Without another mechanism, these errors will accumulate and eventually destroy the system.[126] Feedback mechanisms can compensate for errors over time to maintain effective regulation.[127]

---

[121]Nassim Nicholas Taleb, *The Black Swan: The Impact of the Highly Improbable* (New York: Random House Trade Paperbacks, 2010), xxii.

[122]Heylighen and Joslyn, "Cybernetics and Second Order Cybernetics," 14.

[123]Ibid.

[124]Ibid.

[125]Heylighen, "Principles of Systems and Cybernetics: An Evolutionary Perspective," 7.

[126]Heylighen and Joslyn, "Cybernetics and Second Order Cybernetics," 14.

[127]Ibid.

Feedback or an error controlled mechanism compensates for error or deviation from a goal after it has occurred with the error determining what actions the regulator will take to compensate for it.[128] Feedback provides the mechanism for systems to learn and determine what actions to take to correct deviation from a system's goal or preferred states. Feedback mechanisms increase or decrease a system's variety in order to maintain equilibrium with the environment. If a system's variety has been increased by a disturbance then the regulator will use negative feedback to reduce the amount of variety in the system. If variety in the system needs to be increased then the regulator will use positive feedback to increase the variety or energy in the system. Feedback control mechanism also provides continuity as deviations from goals or errors usually do not appear at once, but tend to increase over time. This gives the regulator the opportunity to intervene at an early stage when the errors are still small.[129]

Therefore effective regulation of a system requires both feedback and feedforward mechanisms. Feedback mechanisms actively compensate for errors or deviations from a goal by increasing or decreasing the variety of a system.[130] Additionally, feedback mechanisms allow a system to adapt to continuous change or disturbances from the environment.[131] Feedforward mechanisms allow a system to cope with discontinuous changes or disturbances that develop so quickly that actions resulting from feedback would not be timely.[132] An effective regulator will consist of a mechanism to cope with both continuous and discontinuous change in the

---

[128]Ibid.

[129]Ibid.

[130]Ibid.

[131]Ibid.

[132]Ibid., 14–15.

environment.[133] The inability for the regulator to discern or detect the small errors or weak signals among the noise will make the system vulnerable because the system may not be able to address error accumulation or the disturbance before it has a significant effect on the system's essential variables.[134]

Figure 2: Control Loop Diagram

Source: Heylighen and Joslyn, "Cybernetics and Second Order Cybernetics," 14.

Therefore, the regulator determines a system's state and organization. The regulator uses the basic mechanism of regulation to learn and regulate. For the sake of clarity and simplicity, the term regulator will be used to refer to what the cybernetics literature has called a control system

---

[133]Ibid., 14.

[134]Ibid.

as they all perform the same basic function of selection and reducing variety.[135] Figure 2 depicts the basic overall scheme of a control loop of a regulator with a feedback cycle with two inputs, the goal and the disturbances.[136] The *system* represents the system or the regulator. The *goal* represents the preferred values of the system's essential variables, while the *disturbances* represents all the processes in the environment that can affect these variables over which the system does not have direct control.[137] The system observes the variables that can affect its preferred state and desires to regulate before the step of *perception* which creates the internal representation of the external situation from the selected *observed variables*.[138] The regulator then processes the *representation* to determine how those variables will affect its *goal* and then determine the requisite action to maintain the goal or preferred state.[139] Based on the interpretation from the *information processing*, the system makes a *decision* to take an appropriate *action* and this *action* affects some part of the environment through the *dynamics* of that environment.[140] An unknown set of variables known as the *disturbance* influences these dynamics and their interaction, in turn, affects the variables in the environment that includes the *observed variables* that the system has selected to observe.[141] Any changes in these *observed variables* is fed into the *perception* step closing the control loop and the *observed variables* usually includes the essential variables that the system must keep within accepted limits and

---

[135]Heylighen, "Principles of Systems and Cybernetics: An Evolutionary Perspective," 7–8.

[136]Heylighen and Joslyn, "Cybernetics and Second Order Cybernetics," 15.

[137]Ibid.

[138]Ibid.

[139]Ibid.

[140]Ibid.

[141]Ibid.

prevent error accumulation through feedback control.[142] The system can also observe various

non-essential variables to anticipate potential disturbances in order to implement feedforward

control.[143] The control loop model is symmetrical, so we can model the interaction with another

system, the object or the environment, by rotating and overlaying another control loop on top as

seen in Figure 3.

Figure 3: Modified Figure 2- Interacting Control Loops

Source: Heylighen and Joslyn, "Cybernetics and Second Order Cybernetics," 16.

This modified control loop model in Figure 3 depicts the interaction between the system

and the object or environment as overlaid control loops. Each control loop has its own goal,

---

[142]Heylighen and Joslyn, "Cybernetics and Second Order Cybernetics," 15–16.

[143]Ibid., 16.

which in turn becomes potential disturbances for the other.[144] If the goals of the two systems do not complement or align with one another, the interaction results in conflict or competition.[145] If the goals of the system and the object complement one another then, interaction results in compromise or cooperation.[146] Regulation requires asymmetry in the control loop, where the actions of the system must have more effect on the state of the environment than environment has on the system. This asymmetry can be achieved by weakening the influence of the environment and by strengthening the actions of the system.[147] A system accomplishes this through learning.

Therefore, equilibrium, from an adaptive systems perspective, equates to The Red Queen principle or the Red Queen Effect.[148] The Red Queen principle is a concept taken from evolutionary theory based on the coadaptive and coevolutionary nature of the systems and its environment.[149] The principle essentially states that the system must keep pace with the rate of change of its environment in order to maintain their current relative position at equilibrium.[150] Which means, the system must create asymmetry in this rate of adaptation in order to establish or maintain a position of relative advantage at equilibrium. Therefore, the system ability to learn while hindering it in competing systems creates this asymmetry in adaptive tempo.

---

[144]Ibid., 16–17.

[145]Ibid., 17.

[146]Ibid.

[147]Ibid.

[148]Ian P McCarthy, "Manufacturing Strategy—Understanding the Fitness Landscape," *International Journal of Operations and Production Management* 24 (2004): 143.

[149]Ibid.

[150]Ibid.

ANALYSIS: ADAPTATION AS A MARKOV PROCESS

Figure 4: Markov Model of Interacting Adaptive Systems

Source: Scott E. Page, "Markov Processes."

This portion of the study will examine Ashby's definition of a self-organizing system, where the system and the environment interact as a bounded whole, and model that interaction as a Markov Process. While the full mathematical treatment of the adaptive process as a Markov model lies beyond the scope of this paper, the study intends to use a Markov model to conceptually represent the interaction between the adaptive systems and its environment as shown in Figure 4. Equifinality, where different initial states lead to the same final state, characterizes goal-seeking systems. This equifinality suggests the equilibrium model of adaptation follows a Markov process and the Markov Convergence theorem. A Markov process is a stochastic process that has a finite number of states, fixed transition probabilities, the possibility of getting from any state to another through a series of transitions, and the system does not produce a simple cycle.[151]

---

[151]Page, "Markov Processes," 76–77.

A stochastic process is a sequence of events in which the outcome at any stage depends on some probability.[152] The Markov Convergence or the Ergodic theorem states a system following a Markov Process will eventually reach a *statistical* equilibrium that does not depend on the initial state of the process or any one time changes to the state during the process.[153] Any process following the Markov Convergence theorem will reach statistical equilibrium given time and the transition probabilities or rates of change and adaptation between two systems remain the same.[154] Statistical equilibrium means that dynamics and the underlying processes continue to occur but transparent as no overall changes in state occur to the system.[155]

The model in Figure 4 depicts the relative change in requisite variety between the system and the object following a Markov process expressed as the transition probabilities p and q. While the arrows in Figure 4 seem to indicate the transfer of requisite variety between the system and the object, in this model it only represents the change in requisite variety due to their interaction. As explained earlier by Ashby's Law of Requisite Variety, requisite variety measures regulation and it must be equal to or larger than the variety of the disturbances in order to maintain stability or equilibrium.[156] Meaning, the control loop with a higher requisite variety can better regulate an exogenous control loop or the environment. Therefore, the transition probabilities can measure the asymmetry between the control loops of the systems as modeled in Figure 3.

---

[152]Page, "Markov Processes."

[153]Ibid., 76-77.

[154]Scott E. Page, "10 - 4 - Markov Convergence Theorem-Model Thinking, " Scott E. Page YouTube, http://www.youtube.com/watch?v=h1hCepx1tQU (accessed 4 April 2014).

[155]Ibid.

[156]Ashby, *An Introduction to Cybernetics*, 247.

According to Ashby, learning determines how well a system can regulate by maintaining

its equilibrium in spite of disturbances and how fast the system returns to relative equilibrium

after a disturbance.[157] Which means, learning determines the transient time of a disturbance

before a system to return to a relative equilibrium. This means goal-seeking adaptive systems

display equifinality, where different initial states still lead to the same final *relative* state at

equilibrium.[158] Therefore, learning or the inability to learn creates the asymmetry in the control

loop and changes the transition probabilities in the model shown in Figure 4. If the transition

probabilities p and q are equal then the relative variety between the system and the object will

also be equal at *statistical* equilibrium. If p or q is greater than the other, then control loop with a

larger transition probability, p for the object and q for the system, will have the greater variety at

statistical equilibrium, therefore a higher level of fitness. So viewed in this way, requisite variety

can measure relative fitness.

Figure 5: Adaptive Processes with Symmetric Transition Probabilities

Source: Scott E. Page, "Markov Processes."

---

[157]Ashby, *Design for a Brain; the Origin of Adaptive Behavior*, 1–9.

[158]Heylighen and Joslyn, "Cybernetics and Second Order Cybernetics," 13.

The transition probability values captures the percentage of variety that the system gains and losses in a cycle or iteration. Figure 5 illustrates an adaptive process as a Markov model with symmetric transition probabilities p and q. At the start, system, expressed below as State 2, has no requisite variety relative to a new environment so begin with a value of 0 and the environment, expressed as State 1, begins with value of 1 to depict the percentage of relative variety. The value of transition probability p and q in this illustration is 0.3. The system reaches an equilibrium after 23 iterations with an equal value of 0.5 or 50 percent for the relative variety of the system and object.

Figure 6: Adaptive Processes with Asymmetric Transition Probabilities

Source: Scott E. Page, "Markov Processes."

Figure 6 illustrates an adaptive process as a Markov model when the asymmetry in transition probabilities favors the system with the value $q = 0.7$ and $p = 0.5$. Again, the system, expressed as State 2, has no requisite variety relative to a new environment, expressed as State 1, so begin with a value of 0 and environment with value of 1 to depict the percentage of relative variety. The system and the object reaches equilibrium at the 14th iteration with the system having a value of .584 or 58.4 percent for relative variety to the value of .416 or 41.6 percent.

Since both models are probabilistic and following a Markov process, initial conditions and inputs into the process, as energy or variety, at any point in this process, as long as the values of the transition probabilities remain the same, the system will return to the same relative equilibrium. The equifinal property of the process does not mean that goal-seeking adaptive systems are not sensitive initial conditions or that inputting energy or variety into the system does not have an effect. As can be seen in the two figures, the start conditions and therefore also the injects of energy to the system, which becomes the new start point, does matter as seen in the amount of the transient time that the process must undergo before it reaches the relative equilibrium point. In order to change or maintain relative advantage at equilibrium, the system must create asymmetry in the transition probabilities, the rate of adaptation and changes. Learning creates this asymmetry.

CASE STUDY 1: NAPOLEON'S GRAND ARMEE (JENA AUERSTADT)

Background and Context

The French Revolution, 1789-91, transformed the armies from private and dynastic armies to national armies.[159] Since the army now served the nation, it had access to unprecedented levels of resources, funds, and troops. Soldiers at all level considered the army as their own and had ideological loyalties to the nation and to the army that served it. With a new abundance of resources the army grew from 180,000 troops in the Bourbon armies in 1789 to over a million in 1794.[160] The new politics of the Revolution abolished the hierarchical caste system and with it the social and political constraints on the actions permitted to the state.

---

[159]Thomas M. Huber, "The Rise of Napoleon," in H100: *Rise of the Western Way of War*, CGSC Academic Year 2012-13, Intermediate Level Education Common Core H104 (Fort Leavenworth, KS: Command and General Staff College, 2012), 87.

[160]Ibid.

Nationalist propaganda and ideology succeeded at creating men of thinking obedience, "not the obedience of slaves, but that of free men."[161] With this army, France waged war on Europe and by late 1790, victory drove the growth of French expansion and nationalism.[162] The upheavals of 1788-94 marked the violent end to entire social, political, and international order in France and eventually to the rest of Europe. The French Revolution brought mass politics and warfare to Europe and ultimately the world.[163] The revolution also freed France and subsequently other nations of the social, economic, and political constraints of the Old Regime. The need to maintain political control and the relative lack of military means kept the aims in Pre-Napoleonic war limited.[164] Francois de Guibert below summarizes the nature of these limited wars and the indecisive nature of battle in the Old Regime in the passage below:

> States have neither treasure nor surplus population. Their expenditures outstrips their revenues even in peace. […] They take the field with armies they can neither recruit nor pay. Victors and vanquished alike are exhausted. […] Often the source of the quarrel is not dried up, and each side sits on its shattered remains while it attempts to pay its debts and sharpen its weapons.[165]

The French strategic and military organization that arose from the Revolution sought to overcome these limitations of the Old Regime by attaining decisive results from war through decisive results in battle. Thus, decisive victory in battle was the goal of the *Grand Armee* and the battle of Jena and Auerstadt serves as clear evidence of its ability to attain that goal. Napoleon makes clear below the purpose of the *Grand Armee*.

---

[161]MacGregor Knox and Williamson Murray, *The Dynamics of Military Revolution, 1300-2050* (Cambridge, UK: Cambridge University Press, 2001), 65.

[162]Ibid., 66–67.

[163]Ibid., 57–58.

[164]Ibid., 58–59.

[165]David G Chandler, *The Campaigns of Napoleon* (New York: Macmillan, 1966), 140.

I only see one thing, namely the enemy's main body. I strive to crush it, confident that secondary matters will then settle themselves.[166]

On 13 September 1806, Prussia invaded Saxony and Napoleon began movement to counter the Prussian advance. The *Grand Armee* crossed the Thuringer Wald in three mutually supported columns through three defiles of the Franconian forest.[167] After minor skirmishes, on 12 October, Napoleon initiated the enveloping maneuver that would lead to the dual battle of Jena-Auerstadt and the defeat of the Prussian army.[168] On 15 October, the battle was joined first at Closewitz and there Napoleon defeated the Prussian force under Hohenlohe at Jena.[169] Only later did Napoleon learn that Marshall Davout's III Corps had singlehandedly defeated the Prussian main army at Auerstadt.[170] This led to the pursuit on 15 October by the *Grand Armee* and ended with the route of the remaining Prussian forces and the surrender of the Prussian commander Kleist. Four days after the surrender of Kleist, Napoleon on the French Army occupied Hamburg ending the Jena-Auerstadt campaign. Over the course of thirty three days of active military campaigning, starting from Saxony,[171] Napoleon and the *Grand Armee* reduced the Prussian Army from a strength of 171,000 to 35,000 and occupied the Prussian capital of Berlin.[172]

---

[166]Ibid., 27.

[167]Michael D Krause and R. Cody Phillips, *Historical Perspectives of the Operational Art* (Washington, DC: Government Printing Office, 2005), 45.

[168]Martin Van Creveld, *Command in War* (Cambridge, MA: Harvard University Press, 1985), 85–87.

[169]Ibid., 93.

[170]Ibid.

[171]Krause and Phillips, *Historical Perspectives of the Operational Art*, 35.

[172]Ibid., 63.

Analysis

The French strategic organization that emerged possessed full national funding, multi-level staffing and planning, and coordinated multiple specialized agencies all sharing one national purpose.[173] Prior to Napoleon's *Grand Armee*, no military forces could operate dispersed on such a large scale with as much uncertainty and still retain the capability for coordinated actions.[174] Some historians propose the ability of the *Grand Armee* to deploy and maneuver large independent forces simultaneously and concentrate them at critical moments in battle represented the emergence of the modern military force.[175] According to these historians, the modern military organization emerged from the Napoleonic Wars in Western Europe from 1792 to 1815 along with many of the organizational features, such as the Napoleonic staff structure, organization, and functions characteristic of modern day armies.[176] Historian David Chandler characterizes the Jena campaign in 1806 as a triumph of Napoleon's novel system of operational art and organization.[177] In fact, Napoleon achieved the victory at Jena and Auerstadt in spite of misidentifying the Prussian main force and leaving only one of his corps, Davout's III corps, on its own to fight it.[178] The ability for the *Grand Armee* to triumph in spite of these shortfalls emerged from the novel organization that allowed it to learn and adjust to the increasing uncertainty of the battlefield that Napoleon's method and pursuit of decisive battle demanded.

---

[173]Huber, "The Rise of Napoleon," 87–88.

[174]Krause and Phillips, *Historical Perspectives of the Operational Art*, 26.

[175]Ibid.

[176]Huber, "The Rise of Napoleon," 87–88.

[177]Krause and Phillips, *Historical Perspectives of the Operational Art*, 65.

[178]Ibid., 64.

The necessary hierarchy formed to accommodate and distribute the uncertainty through multi-level staffing and the combined arms organization of the *corps de armee* which provided the requisite variety to adapt to changes. The *corps de armee* could learn and adjust its organization internally and through mutual support of other corps due to the variety available to them through their operational organization. The *Grand* Armee could fight without having to mass because it could operate and fight as independent and self-contained corps. The thinking obedience of the soldiers and units that composed the *Grand Armee* differentiated it from the other European armies of the time period. This allowed both the preservation of the variety at the subordinate unit level and the structured hierarchy that allowed for control of the units for complex activities without resorting to the rigid tactics and formations of the ancient phalanx or the Prussian "corpse" obedience.[179] Additionally, the organization of the *Grand Armee* permitted the defeat of a single or even multiple corps without necessarily threatening the equilibrium of the *Grand Armee* as a whole. The corps, like the *Grand Armee* itself, were designed as multi-stable and self-organizing systems, possessing their own command and staff and combined arms required to operate independently and dispersed, but able to mass at the decisive point when required by the situation. As Chandler notes, self-sufficiency and mutual support were the keys to the *Grand Armee*'s success.[180]

Systems when confronted with excess variety from the environment can increase its variety or reduce the variety in the environment to achieve regulation. For other nations during Napoleon's time, the regulation of the uncertainty at the subordinate unit level would come by control and reducing the available action of the subordinate elements, such as the rigid uniformity

---

[179]Knox and Murray, *The Dynamics of Military Revolution, 1300-2050*, 61.

[180]Krause and Phillips, *Historical Perspectives of the Operational Art*, 35.

37

imposed on the Prussian units. This forced reduction of the variety reduced significantly the ability of the subordinate units of the Prussian army to cope with changes in their environment, especially those imposed upon it by the *Grand Armee*. Conversely, the *Grand Armee* maximized the variety of its subordinate elements to regulate the disturbances in their environment. To support this, Napoleon grouped divisions and other units flexibly into combined arms army corps that had the capacity to task organize to have the requisite variety for a given engagement. Each corps was designed to be logistically and tactically self-sufficient and had the requisite variety to resist and fight independently for up to two days until it was reinforced, if required, by a mutually supporting corps.[181] Armies of 150,000 to 500,000 men divided into corps that could move dispersed a day or two day's march apart, linked together by cavalry and couriers.[182] The corps had the requisite variety to fight independently and capacity to adapt to a wide variety of disturbances from the environment. Additionally, the mutual support of a supporting corps or Napoleon's own reserve provided additional variety and capabilities to the corps. Flexibility, self-sufficiency, and mutual support made Napoleon's *corps de armee* so effective in the context of its time.

The *bataillon carre*, the battalion of square, was a formation where different corps moved forward abreast along parallel roads across a 120-mile front and connected, as mentioned earlier, by the cavalry and couriers. Napoleon's opponent could not easily maneuver or move out of the way of this advancing 120 mile front thereby permitting Napoleon to force an engagement or avoid them, something novel at the time.[183] This allowed Napoleon to systematically constrain

---

[181]Knox and Murray, *The Dynamics of Military Revolution, 1300-2050*, 66–67.

[182]Ibid., 67.

[183]Huber, "The Rise of Napoleon," 88.

his opponent's options which decreased his uncertainty while simultaneously increasing the uncertainty in his adversary's representation through the use of cavalry and the flexibility of the *Grand Armee*. Tactically, once in the vicinity of the opposing force Napoleon used skirmishers and the assault column to make initial contact with the enemy.[184] Skirmishers were troops that would be deployed forward to fire individually from cover on enemy lines in order to disrupt the formations, creating more internal variety than an enemy system could handle. Once engaged, Napoleon would extend the lines of the *Grand Armee* until all of the enemy had their assets engaged. Then a corps would attack a flank and cause the adversary to reallocate forces in order to defend against the attack. Napoleon would assemble a heavy force, the *force de rupture*, at the point where the enemy line that that had been thinned, which was usually a seam in the line closest to the flanking attack.[185] A sequenced attack of different arms would then follow to break the line. Heavy cavalry attacked causing the adversary lines to form into squares. The infantry or artillery would follow as the cavalry was pulled back to attack with fire on the now massed and compact formation. This would prompt the square to redeploy into a line in order to bring to bear their firepower on the advancing column. Napoleon would repeat this sequence until a gap appeared into the line, to which he would employ the *force de rupture*.[186] Once the rupture had formed, Napoleon would transition immediately to the exploitation of the rupture and the interdiction of the enemy force's lines of communication by his light cavalry. After the loss of general cohesion of the enemy unit, Napoleon would transition to the pursuit by his cavalry to

---

[184]Ibid., 89.

[185]Ibid.

[186]Ibid.

complete the defeat of the enemy force.[187] The flexibility and the freedom of the *Grand Armee* to

transition quickly from one state to another, to include the transition from movement into battle

and back into movement, represents a "sphere" equilibrium which permitted the *Grand Armee* to

adapt and adjust its organization optimally to the disturbances in the environment.

Napoleon also created a multi-level staff system and headquarters to assist in processing

and regulating the complexity of the battlefield.[188] The requisite hierarchy of the multi-level

command staff that formed to deal with the residual variety preserved the variety at the

subordinate level. Napoleon's headquarters, the *grand quartier general* was the component that

enabled Napoleon to employ the *Grand Armee* to its fullest capacity and apply his famed genius

to adapt to the changing battlefield.[189] The *grand quartier general* enabled Napoleon to acquire

and evaluate intelligence from the entire theater of war, control a military front of up to 70 miles,

transmit and receive reports and orders over a large area, and enabling the critical flow of

information to the units of the *Grand Armee*.[190] It was through the *grand quartier general*, multi-

level staffs, and commanders that Napoleon formed the representation that allowed him to learn

and adapt to the changing circumstances of the environment and his adversaries. The

effectiveness of the multi-level staff illustrates the efficacy gained from additional levels of

hierarchy when the environmental variety exceeds the capacity of a control level. Each level

possessed their own commander and staff and the self-contained nature of the *corps de armee*

provided them the capacity to maximally regulate variety. This does not mean that Napoleon did

---

[187]Chandler, *The Campaigns of Napoleon*, 186–190.

[188]Van Creveld, *Command in War*, 96–97.

[189]Ibid.

[190]Krause and Phillips, *Historical Perspectives of the Operational Art*, 29.

not intervene directly to control the corps. Such was the case with Ney's corps near defeat at Jena. Napoleon directly intervened to prevent the destruction of Ney's corps.[191] Overall, this hierarchy consisting of multiple levels of commanders and staff permitted the *Grand Armee* to regulate the uncertainty and possible variations on the battlefield without having to reduce the variety and freedom for its subordinate elements.

Conclusion

As the case study has demonstrated, the organization and structure of Napoleon's *Grand Armee* as a system was exceedingly effective in attaining decisive victory in battle. The *Grand Armee*'s performance demonstrated the effectiveness of its organization to deal with and adjust to the uncertainty on the battlefield. It provided Napoleon the variety of actions to adjust to changing circumstances in the environment as well as presenting rapidly changing circumstances to their adversaries. This would create the asymmetry of requisite variety to produce decisive victory for Napoleon in *battle*. Napoleon and the *Grand Armee* decisively defeated the Prussian military at Jena-Auerstadt and in subsequent campaigns. Yet the overwhelming victory and the capturing of the Prussian capital did not yield the desired political conditions. Prussia could still function politically, though much degraded, without its army. The original Prussian goal may have been the defeat of the French Army and the reestablishment of their dominance on the European continent.[192] However, after the decisive defeat of their army and the loss of their capital reduced this to a more fundamental goal of survival and with it, the change of their essential variables. The French Revolution and all of its implications created the conditions for war to transition from conflict between monarchs and armies to conflicts between nations.

---

[191]Ibid., 65.

[192]Ibid., 36–39.

Historians assert that the French revolution and the wars conducted by France and its enemies from 1792 to 1814 became the first war between nations.[193] Mass politics and fanaticism removed all theoretical limits to the aims and methods of warfare.[194] In short, it approached Clausewitz's formulation of absolute war.

> [W]ar… again became the affair of the people as a whole, and took on an entirely different character, or rather approached its true character, its absolute perfection.[195]

Therefore with war becoming an affair of the nation and people as a whole and not just the monarchs, nobility, and their armies, war took on an entirely different character as Clausewitz notes here. As war became the affair of the people and not just the army, decisive victory in battle would no longer produce decisive results in war. As battles became decisive, the necessity of campaigns, or the linking of a series of decisive battles, to achieve strategic results provides the evidence of the initial adaptation and learning by the system in reducing the significance of single battle to a series of battles. This adaptation would continue as campaigns became the primary source of disturbance. Nations would eventually adapt and become multi-stable systems with the military being only one of the instruments of national power that could maintain its equilibrium. Ironically while the social, economic, and political changes of the French Revolution provided the capability to produce decisive results on the battlefield, it also set the conditions to reduce the decisiveness of battle in war.

---

[193]Knox and Murray, *The Dynamics of Military Revolution, 1300-2050*, 58.

[194]Ibid.

[195]Clausewitz, *On War*, 563.

CASE STUDY 2: AL QUAEDA (POST 9-11 TO CURRENT)

Background and Context

Al Qaeda (AQ) has evolved into a significantly different terrorist organization since their execution of the 11 September 2001 attacks. At the time, a core cadre of veterans of the Afghan insurgency against the Soviet Union formed a centralized leadership structure and a majority of the organization's plans and direction emanated from the top or approved by the leadership.[196] According to US officials, Al Qaeda cells and associates are now located in over 70 countries and these individuals never leave their home country but are radicalized by others who have traveled abroad for training and indoctrination through the use of modern transportation and communications technology.[197] The name "Qaeda" means "base" or "foundation," upon which its members hope to build a robust and geographically diverse network.[198] Out of necessity, due to pressures from global counter-terrorism effort, Al Qaeda has transformed into a diffuse global network and philosophical movement of semi-independent and dispersed nodes. While degraded, some experts consider Al Qaeda's development in the recent years makes them more difficult to target and potentially more lethal.[199] A Congressional Research Service (CRS) report stated that according to senior US government officials, Al Qaeda has become increasingly decentralized and possesses shifting centers of gravity.[200] Seth Jones stated, in a testimony to Congress, that

---

[196]John Rollins et al., *Al Qaeda and Affiliates Historical Perspective, Global Presence, and Implications for U.S. Policy* (Washington, DC: Congressional Research Service, 2010), Summary, http://www.fas.org/sgp/crs/terror/R41070.pdf (accessed 9 April 2014).

[197]Ibid., 6-7.

[198]Ibid.

[199]Ibid., Summary.

[200]Ibid.

present day Al Qaeda is organized into four tiers: central Al Qaeda, affiliated groups, allied groups, and inspired networks.[201]

The organization's senior leadership in Pakistan led by Ayman al-Zawahiri compose the first tier of central Al Qaeda. This first tier maintains the oversight, adjudicates disputes among affiliates, and provides strategic guidance.[202] The affiliated groups compose the second tier and these groups have become formal branches of Al Qaeda, with their leaders swearing *bayat* or loyalty to Al Qaeda leaders in Pakistan.[203] These organizations include Al Qaeda in Iraq (AQI) based in Iraq, Al Qaeda in the Arabian Peninsula (AQAP) in Yemen, al Shabaab in Somalia, Al Qaeda in the Islamic Maghreb (AQIM) in Algeria and neighboring countries, and the most recent affiliate, Jabhat al-Nusrah, based in Syria.[204] Allied groups form the third tier and these groups have established a direct relationship with Al Qaeda, but have not yet become formal members. This arrangement allows the groups to remain independent and pursue their own goals, while still working with Al Qaeda when interests and goals align.[205] Finally, the inspired networks form the bottom tier and these groups have no direct contact to Al Qaeda central, but inspired by the Al Qaeda cause. They tend to be motivated by a hatred of the West and their allied regimes in the Middle East.[206]

---

[201]Seth G. Jones, "Re-Examining the Al Qa'ida Threat to the United States" (Rand Corporation, 18 July 2013), 5, http://www.rand.org/pubs/testimonies/CT396-1.html (accessed 9 April 2014).

[202]Ibid.

[203]Ibid., 5–6.

[204]Ibid., 6.

[205]Ibid.

[206]Ibid., 6–7.

Overall, statements from Al Qaeda leadership from the mid-1990s through the present suggest their stated goal is to serve as the vanguard of an international Islamist movement that inspires Muslims and other individuals to help defend and purify Islam through violent means. These statements advocate for a phased struggle, with the initial goal of the expulsion of US and foreign military forces from Islamic lands which would then lead to the proximate goals to overthrow of corrupt regional leaders and the formation of governments ruled exclusively according to sharia or Islamic law.[207] References frequently appear in Al Qaeda propaganda of the stated goal of reestablishing an Islamic caliphate, but often lack detail and any practical political prescriptions for achieving such a goal. In fact, some experts now argue that Al Qaeda has become a marginal actor in international Islamist militancy.[208]

<u>Analysis</u>

Since 11 September, an interest has developed into the organizational functioning of Al-Qaeda and the wider movement of radical Islamist militancy and terrorism. The ambiguous and diffused nature of Al Qaeda and their resiliency to military efforts has invited research in the efficacy of their organizational structure. To some, the diffused network and virtually leaderless organization of Al Qaeda embodies the essence of self-organizing, complex adaptive systems. Colonel Michael Beech in his paper, *Observing Al Qaeda Through the Lens of Complexity Theory*, describes Al Qaeda as a decentralized and polymorphic network with geographical and functional dispersion across associated terrorist organizations able to adapt and aggregate in

---

[207]Rollins et al., *Al Qaeda and Affiliates Historical Perspective, Global Presence, and Implications for U.S. Policy*, 29–30.

[208]Ibid., 29.

pursuit of common interests and goals.[209] According Marion and Uhl-Bien, self-organization of Al Qaeda and the emergence of its leadership results from interactive non-linear bottom up dynamics. They claim that leaders do not create the system or organization, but the system creates the leaders through the process of emergence.[210] Marion and Uhl-Bien describe Al Qaeda as a moderately coupled network that can adjust as required by the circumstances and their activities, post 9-11, demonstrates the organizational efficacy of a virtually leaderless and non-hierarchical network structure.[211] Even in the 11 September 2001 attacks, testimonies reportedly indicated that high level Al Qaeda leadership had been minimally informed and had a limited role in directing the operation.[212] Author Antoine Bousquet asserts that this form of organization confounds Western states and their hierarchical security organizations. Bousquet highlights the ability of the Al Qaeda network to function and avoid defeat by the United States and its allies as a demonstration of the resilience and adaptability of their network organization.[213] Despite the cited efficacies of their network organization, the inability of Al Qaeda to make any gains towards their stated goal or coordinate the activities of their organization above the tactical level clearly indicates the limitations of their organizational structure.

The lack of details and inability to coordinate an effort may be the result of the AQ network not having enough hierarchy to coordinate and integrate enough of its affiliates and

---

[209]Michael F Beech, "Observing Al Qaeda through the Lens of Complexity Theory: Recommendations for the National Strategy to Defeat Terrorism" (USAWC Strategy Research Project, U.S. Army War College, 2004).

[210]Russ Marion and Mary Uhl-Bien, "Complexity Theory and Al-Qaeda: Examining Complex Leadership," *Emergence* 5, no. 1 (2003): 59–60.

[211]Ibid., 58–60.

[212]Bousquet, *The Scientific Way of Warfare*, 208.

[213]Ibid., 209.

supporters to conduct the actions at that level. As an example of this fragmentation, AQI leaders utilized their established networks in Syria to establish Jabhat al-Nusrah as their operational arm as the conflict in Syria began to intensify in 2011.[214] Eventually, Jabhat al-Nusrah established its own sources of funding, fighters, and material, it became increasingly independent from AQI. Asserting his independence from Al Qaeda in Iraq, Jabhat al-Nusrah leader Abu Muhammad al-Jawlani declared his loyalty directly to Al Qaeda's central leadership in Pakistan April 2013.[215] These kinds of internal competition and conflicts among the sub-systems of Al Qaeda shows the cost of so called leaderless network organization and the lack of requisite hierarchy of the Al Qaeda "leadership" to regulate these internal disturbances.

Evidence also exists that Al Qaeda have challenges in attracting support due to differences, often conflicting, in the representation of the organization and the goals created by the incompatibility of different components of Al Qaeda's ideology and organization. Al Qaeda and its regional affiliates appeal for support based on a wide range of political positions and often conflicting agendas.[216] These differing priorities, approaches, and contexts challenges Al Qaeda in creating a unified and coherent narrative and strategy. According to some experts, even Al Qaeda's representation of their enemy has been inconsistent and confusing, another indicator that Al Qaeda may lack an overall strategy.[217] Reportedly, Al Qaeda's various operational units, affiliates or inspired networks, mix and match elements from various ideological and strategic

---

[214]Jones, "Re-Examining the Al Qa'ida Threat to the United States," 8–9.

[215]Ibid., 6.

[216]Rollins et al., *Al Qaeda and Affiliates Historical Perspective, Global Presence, and Implications for U.S. Policy*, 30.

[217]Ibid.

documents to identify elements that they can achieve.[218] Organizationally, this describes Al Qaeda's subsystems conducting BVSR, using trial and error to come to the requisite variety or knowledge to achieve the higher organization's goals. As noted earlier, the more complex the environment becomes, the less probable that the system will select and retain the requisite variety. This severely constrains Al Qaeda's ability to achieve their stated policy goals or any true coordinated action. Conversely, this dispersed nature makes the organization very resilient and difficult to target as a whole.[219]

Conclusion

The resilience to direct regulation and action has typically been the cited merits of Al Qaeda's network and non-hierarchical organization, but it also constrains their ability to coordinate and act cohesively. It took over three years to plan and execute the attacks of 9-11 by Al Qaeda and the effectiveness of their attack may have arisen more from the United States' surprise and lack of anticipation of such an attack. Had the United States anticipated it, the relatively simple attack could have been easily thwarted. The security measures and the counterterrorism efforts undertaken by the United States clearly shows the learning and the reestablishment of asymmetry in response to those attacks. Thus far Al Qaeda has not displayed any indications of effectively addressing this asymmetry.

The Al Qaeda movement has become a more diffuse movement today as a necessary adaptation to the current counterterrorism efforts. The growth in the number and geographic scope of Al Qaeda affiliates and allies over the past decade indicates that Al Qaeda as a brand

---

[218]Ibid.

[219]Ibid.

name remains relevant and a threat.[220] The growing Sunni-Shi'a struggle across the Middle East provides fertile ground and resources for Sunni militant groups like Al Qaeda.[221] Yet, despite this dispersion and the influence of the Al Qaeda network, this aspect of their organization also hinders their ability to act and cope with even a relatively small amount of complexity and variety. As the network grows more dispersed and adapts to direct counterterrorist activities, experts have noted the struggle against the Al Qaeda movement will transition predominantly to an *ideological* struggle.[222] The decisions made by regional governments highlight the relative importance of combating Al Qaeda operatives, affiliates, and ideologues within their own societies which will ultimately determine the efficacy and long term influence of Al Qaeda.[223] Experts cite recent indications of the effectiveness of US and allied counterterrorism policies when capitalizing on Al Qaeda actions that alienate current or potential supporters. Similarly, in response, Al Qaeda members seek to capitalize on US and allied policies and actions unpopular among Muslim audiences, targeting unfavorable tactical actions as well as broader policies such as the presence of foreign military forces in Muslim countries. Thus "war" against Al Qaeda will seemingly remain predominantly a war of ideas and ideology rather than a war of military action.[224]

---

[220]Ibid., 31–32.

[221]Ibid.

[222]Jones, "Re-Examining the Al Qa'ida Threat to the United States," 12.

[223]Rollins et al., *Al Qaeda and Affiliates Historical Perspective, Global Presence, and Implications for U.S. Policy*, 31–32.

[224]Antulio Joseph Echevarria, *Wars of Ideas and the War of Ideas* (Carlisle, PA: U.S. Army War College, 2008), v–vi.

CONCLUSIONS

Thus it is said that one who knows the enemy and knows himself will not be endangered in a hundred engagements. One who does not know the enemy but knows himself will sometimes be victorious, sometimes meet with defeat. One who knows neither the enemy nor himself will invariably be defeated in every engagement.[225]

Uncertainty drives creativity and adaptability in systems. Without the driver of uncertainty and variety in the environment, systems would not have a mechanism for learning, adaptation, and innovation once they reach equilibrium as the basic tendency of any system is stability.[226] As noted by Wieck, certainty can constrain and inhibit action, creativity, learning, and adaptation.[227] This study concludes that living, goal seeking systems can change the rates of adaptation, expressed as transition probabilities, through learning to produce a favorable asymmetry so that the system has a position of relative advantage at equilibrium. Since uncertainty can contain potentially unlimited possibilities of variety in the product space, constraint in some form to that variety is required in order for a system to anticipate and conduct regulation. Therefore, identification and retention of the knowledge of these constraints improves a system's ability to learn and adjust its organization accordingly. The identification of these constraints occurs in the *representation* step of the control loop in Figure 3.

Representation of the external situation drives what the system learns and ultimately adapts to. As Sun Tzu states the better representation a system has of itself and of the object increases its ability to regulate, which in this instance means the attainment of victory in war. So

---

[225]Sun Tzu, *Art of War*, ed. Ralph Sawyer and Mei- Chün Sawyer (Boulder, CO: Westview Press, 1994), 179.

[226]Ashby and Goldstein, "Principles of Self-Organizing Systems," 118.

[227]Weick, *Sensemaking in Organizations*, 59–61.

with this representation, systems can create favorable asymmetry in the control loop by learning and regulating the environment to affect the learning of the object. Stuart Umpleby suggested instead of changing the object directly, changing the environment of the object such that the interaction rules between the object and its environment changes the object in the desired direction.[228] By shaping the representation of the external situation, the system affects the learning and adaptation of the object so that it behaves in a desired manner. As Sun Tzu advises from the Art of War, "Warfare is the Way (Tao) of deception."[229]

A system's strategy or plan is its representation of the external situation and its anticipated actions based on anticipated conditions. Which means that by shaping the enemy's perception and therefore his representation of the external world, we can regulate their plans and actions to our favor. Again, as Sun Tzu advises, the key then is to attack the enemy's strategy or plan,[230] to attack their representation since it drives both learning and adaptation, thereby creating the favorable asymmetry for the system and enabling a system to create discontinuous change or disturbance so that the object could not adapt or learn in a timely manner.[231] This concept describes essentially what Boyd had referred to as getting inside of an opponent's OODA Loop.

---

[228]Umpleby, "Ross Ashby's General Theory of Adaptive Systems," 8.

[229]Sun Tzu, *Art of War*, 168.

[230]Ibid., 177.

[231]Heylighen and Joslyn, "Cybernetics and Second Order Cybernetics," 14-15.

Figure 7: Boyd's Observation, Orientation, Decision, and Action (OODA) Loop[232]

Source: Osinga, *Science, Strategy and War the Strategic Theory of John Boyd*, 232.

Boyd also states that the goal is to generate mental images or impressions that correspond to that world and that ability was the key to winning versus losing.[233] Boyd argues that the ultimate aim is to create and perpetuate a fluid and menacing state of affairs for the enemy, and to disrupt or incapacitate their ability to adapt to such an environment.[234] The OODA loop, depicted in Figure 7, is a cybernetic control loop, as depicted in Figure 3, with the steps of representation and information processing encompassed in Boyd's conceptualization of orientation. Boyd asserts that the OODA loop is less a model of decision making than a model of individual and organizational learning and adaptation. Boyd also acknowledges the critical role orientation plays in the adaptation and learning of a system.[235]

---

[232]Osinga, *Science, Strategy and War the Strategic Theory of John Boyd*, 232.

[233]Ibid.

[234]Ibid., 236.

[235]Ibid., 235.

This study determined goal seeking systems have a range of goals and possess the capacity of *adapting* those goals, when their essential variables are threatened.[236] This leads to an interesting perspective in viewing centers of gravity of a system. Given the diverse and wide variance of interpretation of the center of gravity, the study focuses not on connecting it to a preexisting concept or definition, but to offer a potential connection to the cybernetic conceptualization of essential variables. Systems maintain overall equilibrium by regulating the variety on these few essential variables from disturbances. Therefore, disturbing these essential variables out of their accepted range a system can cause an object to adapt by changing its essential variables, which in turn changes its goals. The intent then would be to affect those essential variables in manner that the adversary adopts a goal advantageous to us or that they establish an unfavorable equilibrium. Additionally, this could also account for the dynamic shifting centers of gravity observed in adversary systems when conditions in the environment change. These observations may be the adversary's system changing their goals and their associated essential variables in order reestablish equilibrium.

In relation to the phenomenon of war, this phenomenon produces an interesting insight through the case studies. Since disturbance that pushes a system from equilibrium represents a change of organization, all dynamic systems will change their internal organizations spontaneously until they reach a stable equilibrium.[237] Once systems adapt to the disturbance that "broke" it, the system now has the ability to maintain stable equilibrium despite the presence of the disturbance. Ashby concluded that a system's continued existence or persistence proved that it

---

[236] Ashby, *An Introduction to Cybernetics*, 247.

[237] Asaro, "From Mechanisms of Adaptation to Intelligence Amplifiers," 159.

had achieved a stable equilibrium.[238] With this context in mind, in the case of Napoleon, the *Grand Armee* broke the European Old Regime's way of war at the time through the achievement of decisive battle. The initial learning and adaptation of the system would lead to the advent of campaigns where not single, but a series of decisive battle would be required to defeat an adversary and achieve strategic objectives. As the war between armies transitioned to a war between nations, the other nations continued to learn and adapt to the political, social, and economic changes brought on by the French Revolution and the Napoleonic Wars and would eventually allow them to reestablish a stable equilibrium. As the nations became increasingly stable and multi-stable systems over time, decisive battle and military campaigns alone began to have less of an effect because the nations, as a system, adapted and learned and the military was no longer the sole instrument of national power capable of maintaining a nation's equilibrium. So, while battle would become more decisive, the adaptation of the overall system would make war through solely military means less decisive as nations would learn and adapt to maintain stable equilibrium in spite of the disturbance caused by battle and military means. Boyd makes the observation that Western commanders focus overly on the winning of battles.[239]

As seen in the Al Qaeda case study, the learning to cope with the increasingly effective military means of nations such as the United States resulted in organizations adapted to operate in spite of them and resorting to wars of ideas to achieve equilibrium. Antulio Joseph Echevarria defines a war of ideas as a clash of visions, concepts, and images, and their interpretations.[240] Echevarria states wars of ideas are wars because they serve a political, socio-cultural, or economic purpose, and involve hostile intentions or acts. Even though the physical violence may

---

[238]Ibid.

[239]Osinga, *Science, Strategy and War the Strategic Theory of John Boyd*, 143.

[240]Echevarria, *Wars of Ideas and the War of Ideas*, v.

be minimal, Echevarria states we must understand wars of ideas as a mode of conflict and still recognize that physical events, by designed or incidental, are still important to the determination of the course and outcome of a war of ideas.[241] Such with the case of Al Qaeda, the inability to consistently represent themselves and their environment through their ideas, concepts, images, and their actions have led to their recent diminished capacity.

According to Sun Tzu, "subjugating the enemy's army without fighting is the true pinnacle of excellence."[242] With all of the potential variation in our complex environment, the pinnacle of excellence may lie in the ability to shape the representation and learning of an adversary so they change states or adopt goals in a manner that provides us a position of relative advantage and achieve our strategic aims.

---

[241]Ibid., vi-ix.

[242]Sun Tzu, *Art of War*, 177.

BIBLIOGRAPHY

Asaro, Peter M. "From Mechanisms of Adaptation to Intelligence Amplifiers: The Philosophy of W. Ross Ashby." *Mechanical Mind in History.* (2008): 149–184.

Ashby, R., and J. Goldstein. "Principles of Self-Organizing Systems" (Originally Published in 1962). *Emergence : Complexity and Organization* 6, no. 1/2 (2004): 102–126.

Ashby, W. Ross. *An Introduction to Cybernetics.* New York: J. Wiley, 1956.

————. *Design for a Brain; the Origin of Adaptive Behavior.* New York: J. Wiley, 1960.

Beech, Michael F. "Observing Al Qaeda through the Lens of Complexity Theory: Recommendations for the National Strategy to Defeat Terrorism." USAWC Strategy Research Project, U.S. Army War College, 2004.

Bousquet, Antoine J. *The Scientific Way of Warfare: Order and Chaos on the Battlefields of Modernity.* New York: Columbia University Press, 2009.

Chandler, David G. *The Campaigns of Napoleon.* New York: Macmillan, 1966.

Chairman, Joint Chiefs of Staff. Joint Publication (JP) 3-0, *Joint Operations.* Washington, DC: Government Printing Office, 2011.

Chris Lucas. "Perturbation and Transients—The Edge of Chaos." http://www.calresco. org/perturb.htm (accessed 7 April 2014).

Clausewitz, Carl von. *On War.* Edited by Michael Howard, and Peter Paret. Princeton, NJ: Princeton University Press, 1976.

Cliff Joslyn, and Francis Heylighen. "Variety. " Principia Cybernetica Web, 2001. http://pespmc1.vub.ac.be/VARIETY.html. (accessed 13 April 2014).

Echevarria, Antulio Joseph. *Wars of Ideas and the War of Ideas.* Carlisle, PA: U.S. Army War College, 2008, v–vi. http://purl.access.gpo.gov/GPO/LPS95756 (accessed 24 April 2014).

Heylighen, Francis. "Principles of Systems and Cybernetics: An Evolutionary Perspective." *Cybernetics and Systems* 92 (1992): 3–10.

Heylighen, Francis, and Cliff Joslyn. "Cybernetics and Second Order Cybernetics." Edited by R. A. Myers. *Encyclopedia of Physical Science & Technology,* 3rd ed. New York: Academic Press, 2001.

Huber, Thomas M. "The Rise of Napoleon." In H100: *Rise of the Western Way of War*, 87–91. CGSC Academic Year 2012-13. Intermediate Level Education Common Core H104. Fort Leavenworth, KS: United States Command and General Staff College, 2012.

Jones, Seth G. "Re-Examining the Al Qa'ida Threat to the United States." Rand Corporation, 18 July 2013. http://www.rand.org/pubs/testimonies/CT396-1.html (accessed 13 April 2014).

Knox, MacGregor, and Williamson Murray. *The Dynamics of Military Revolution, 1300-2050.* Cambridge, UK: Cambridge University Press, 2001.

Krause, Michael D., and R. Cody Phillips. *Historical Perspectives of the Operational Art.* Washington, DC: Government Printing Office, 2005.

Marion, Russ, and Mary Uhl-Bien. "Complexity Theory and Al-Qaeda: Examining Complex Leadership." *Emergence* 5, no. 1 (2003): 54–76.

McCarthy, Ian P. "Manufacturing Strategy—Understanding the Fitness Landscape." *International Journal of Operations and Production Management* 24 (2004): 124–150.

Osinga, Frans P. B. *Science, Strategy and War the Strategic Theory of John Boyd.* New York: Routledge, 2007.

Page, Scott E. "10—4—Markov Convergence Theorem-Model Thinking. Scott E. Page, YouTube." http://www.youtube.com/watch?v=h1hCepx1tQU (accessed 4 April 2014).

———. "Markov Processes," n.d. http://vserver1.cscs.lsa.umich.edu/~spage/ONLINECOURSE/ R10Markov.pdf (accessed 4 April 2014).

Rollins, John. *Al Qaeda and Affiliates Historical Perspective, Global Presence, and Implications for U.S. Policy.* Washington, DC: Congressional Research Service, 2010. http://www.fas.org/sgp/crs/terror/R41070.pdf (accessed 9 April 2014).

Sun Tzu. *Art of War.* Edited by Ralph D Sawyer and Mei-Chün Sawyer. Boulder, CO: Westview Press, 1994.

Taleb, Nassim Nicholas. *Antifragile: Things That Gain from Disorder.* New York: Random House, 2012.

———. *The Black Swan: The Impact of the Highly Improbable.* New York: Random House Trade Paperbacks, 2010.

Umpleby, S. A. "Ross Ashby's General Theory of Adaptive Systems." *International Journal of General Systems* 38, no. 2 (2009): 231–238.

University of Colorado at Boulder. "Understanding Our Environment—Niche_Modelling.pdf," n.d. http://culter.colorado.edu/~kittel/Biogeog_lectures/ L4b_niche/ Niche_Modelling.pdf (accessed 4 April 2014).

Van Creveld, Martin. *Command in War.* Cambridge, MA: Harvard University Press, 1985.

Weick, Karl E. "Organizing and Sensemaking." *Organizational Behavior* 2 (2006): 90.

———. *Sensemaking in Organizations.* Thousand Oaks: Sage Publications, 1995.